Parables
OF JESUS

www.iCharacter.org

Published by iCharacter Limited ®. (Ireland)
By Agnes de Bezenac
Illustrated by Agnes de Bezenac
Colored by Henny Y.
All Bible verses adapted from the KJV.

Copyright © 2020 by iCharacter Limited ®. All rights reserved. No part of this book may be reproduced in any form or by any electronic or mechanical means, including information storage and retrieval systems, without written permission from the publisher or author, except in the case of a reviewer, who may quote brief passages embodied in critical articles or in a review.

What is a parable?

A parable is a simple story that teaches a lesson. Jesus told many parables, to big people and to little people. We can follow good examples from these parables to live a happy life.

Help! Help!

A man was traveling far from home. When suddenly, robbers attacked him. They beat him up and took his money and clothes. The man lay on the road, very hurt. Ouch! He needed help. Some people passed by. They stopped to look, but then just walked away. Finally, a helpful man came by. He stopped to look and he stopped to help. He bandaged the man's cuts and gave him something to drink. The helpful man took him to a safe place to rest and get better.

Jesus, I also want to stop and help others. Please help me to do the loving thing.

Growing seeds

A farmer went out to plant a garden. The seeds blew with the wind all over the place. Whoosh! Some seeds fell on the dirt road, but the birds ate them up. Peck, Peck! Some fell on rocks, but they soon dried up. Some fell in the middle of weeds and got covered up and choked. Cough, cough! But the other seeds fell on good ground. These grew into strong plants that grew good food.

Jesus, help me to listen to your Word and to do what it says.

Too much

There was a rich man who had many fields and grew lots of food. He stored the food in barns. But there was so much food that his barns were full and no more food could fit in. Could he share some of the food? Yes! Did he share some of the food? No! "I will build bigger barns and keep it all for myself." he said. But soon he died. And all his stuff didn't do him any good. It could have turned out a lot better if he shared.

Jesus, I have many blessings. Please help me to share what I have with others.

Where are you?

A shepherd took his sheep for a walk in the fields for some yummy green grass and cool water. Then he led them to a safe place for the night. But as he counted his sheep... one was missing! "Oh no. I need to find my lost sheep." said the shepherd. He searched the hills, the valleys, the rocks, the bushes. And finally... "There you are!". The shepherd carried his sheep safely home. She was lost, but now was found.

Thank you Jesus, for being our best shepherd. You rescue us when we get lost.

Miracles OF JESUS

What is a miracle?

A miracle is something impossible that only God's power can do. Jesus did many miracles while he was on earth.

Learning about them helps our faith in God to grow stronger.

I can see!

Imagine everything black and dark, nothing to see, nowhere to go. No books to read or no videos to watch. This is what it's like to be blind.

One day, a blind man sat by the road. As Jesus walked by, the man cried "Please heal me. Please help me see!" Jesus knelt down and touched the man's eyes. The man slowly opened his eyes and... he could see! He could see!

Thank you Jesus, for the miracle of sight. I am blessed because I have two eyes to see.

Little girl, get up!

A little girl lay in bed, so very sick. She didn't move or even open her eyes. Her family cried and cried. There was nothing they could do to help her. So they asked Jesus for help. Jesus came to her bedside and took her hand. "Little girl, get up!" The little girl moved, opened her eyes, and then got up. She was all better again! "Thank you, Jesus." They said, as they cried for joy.

I am blessed because I can run, jump and play. Thank you Jesus for good health.

The biggest picnic ever

One day, Jesus spoke to a big crowd of people. Many hours later, the people got hungry. But only one boy had brought his picnic lunch along. "Here, you can have my food," he said to Jesus.

Jesus took the picnic lunch and prayed. "Give some to everyone!" he said. So little food for so many people? Yes! There was enough food to feed the whole crowd. What a miracle! This was the biggest picnic ever, and they even had leftovers.

I am blessed because I have food to eat each day. Thank you Jesus for the miracle of supply.

A mighty storm

Splash, crash! There was a big rain storm. The waves crashed and splashed on the little boat. Everything was soaking wet. "We're gonna sink!" shouted Jesus' helpers. Jesus was sleeping on the boat. He was not afraid. "Wake up Jesus! Help us! We're going to die in this storm." they said. Jesus stood up and said, "Wind, waves and rain, calm down!" Suddenly, all was peaceful again.

I don't have to fear, because Jesus is with me.
Thank you Jesus for the miracle of peace.

More from iCharacter.org

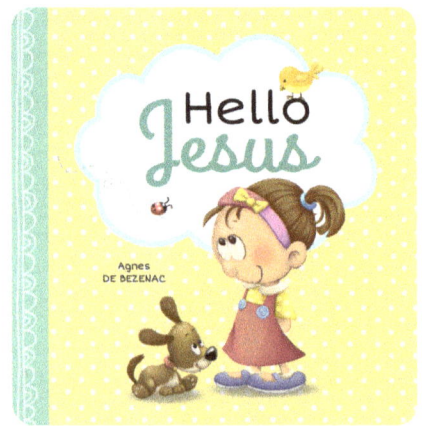 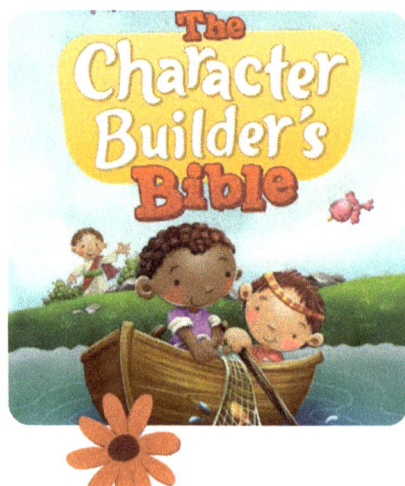 

www.ingramcontent.com/pod-product-compliance
Lightning Source LLC
Chambersburg PA
CBHW040013080526
44586CB00028B/2993